1,000,000 Books

are available to read at

Forgotten Books

www.ForgottenBooks.com

Read online
Download PDF
Purchase in print

ISBN 978-1-334-68314-5
PIBN 10745087

This book is a reproduction of an important historical work. Forgotten Books uses
state-of-the-art technology to digitally reconstruct the work, preserving the original format
whilst repairing imperfections present in the aged copy. In rare cases, an imperfection in
the original, such as a blemish or missing page, may be replicated in our edition. We do,
however, repair the vast majority of imperfections successfully; any imperfections that
remain are intentionally left to preserve the state of such historical works.

Forgotten Books is a registered trademark of FB &c Ltd.
Copyright © 2018 FB &c Ltd.
FB &c Ltd, Dalton House, 60 Windsor Avenue, London, SW19 2RR.
Company number 08720141. Registered in England and Wales.

For support please visit www.forgottenbooks.com

1 MONTH OF FREE READING

at

www.ForgottenBooks.com

By purchasing this book you are eligible for one month membership to ForgottenBooks.com, giving you unlimited access to our entire collection of over 1,000,000 titles via our web site and mobile apps.

To claim your free month visit:
www.forgottenbooks.com/free745087

* Offer is valid for 45 days from date of purchase. Terms and conditions apply.

English
Français
Deutsche
Italiano
Español
Português

www.forgottenbooks.com

Mythology Photography **Fiction**
Fishing Christianity **Art** Cooking
Essays Buddhism Freemasonry
Medicine **Biology** Music **Ancient Egypt** Evolution Carpentry Physics
Dance Geology **Mathematics** Fitness
Shakespeare **Folklore** Yoga Marketing
Confidence Immortality Biographies
Poetry **Psychology** Witchcraft
Electronics Chemistry History **Law**
Accounting **Philosophy** Anthropology
Alchemy Drama Quantum Mechanics
Atheism Sexual Health **Ancient History**
Entrepreneurship Languages Sport
Paleontology Needlework Islam
Metaphysics Investment Archaeology
Parenting Statistics Criminology
Motivational

DEDICATION.
To H.M.

True son of Eton, you who stand
   A guardian to her golden store,
To guide her torch from hand to hand,
   In Peace a Happy Warrior.

You loved the glories which endure
   Of all those Grecian glories gone;
You loved the strong, the sane, the pure,
   And love the more to hand them on.

You saw the vision glorious
   And strove to bring that vision true,
To have your Eton live in us,
   As all our Eton lives in you.

Seeing not only all the best,
   But thinking not a worse can be,
And blest as only they are blest,
   Who dare the strength of trust to see.

We have not skill nor fame to boast:
   You are a poet; you have known
What first we sing we prize the most,
   So take this from us, for your own.

                                       D. S. B.

DEDICATION.
To H.M.

Since you gave us, sir, to know
    All the Muses' golden store,
And a treasure rich did shew,
    Hidden from our souls before.

Since in long past days of peace
    You spread forth before our gaze
Wonder-working things of Greece,
    Filling us with glad amaze.

We, in these hard days of war,
    Turn a little back our eyes
For the things we loved before
    Still our anxious souls must prize.

We this little garland bring
    To your feet, and pray you " take,"
Not for worth of that we sing,
    But for Mother Eton's sake.

                              C. J. S. S.

CONTENTS.

	PAGE
Three Dedications	
VICTOR TAIT PEROWNE—	
A Dirge	1
Founder's Ode	3
Two Sonnets	5
A Picture	7
To Cecilia	9
RICHARD DICKINSON—	
After the French of Estienne de la Boétie	10
FRANCIS BISHOP—	
Fancy	11
ARTHUR RHYS-DAVIDS—	
In Memoriam	12
Thoughts	14
Lines on Hearing Beethoven's "Moonlight" Sonata	15
H. G. M.—	
To R. W.	17
Death	18

		PAGE
CECIL SPRIGGE—		
On an Early Morning Funeral in Amiens Cathedral		19
Beggars in Lyonesse. I.		20
,, ,, II.		21
Le Suicide		22
Lines		23
The Home-Coming. I.		24
,, ,, II.		25
In Memoriam		26
ANON.—		
Literary Fancies		28
Summer		29
My Home		30
PERCY MARYON-WILSON—		
Requiescam		31
Nec quae praeterit hora redire potest		32
THORVALD CAROE—		
Beatus ille		33
ANON.—		
The Prisoner		34
Life		35
DENIS S. BUXTON—		
Vale		36

A DIRGE.

Thou art no longer here.
No longer shall we see thy face,
But, in that other place,
Where may be heard
The roar of the world rushing down the want-ways of the stars;
And the silver bars
Of Heaven's gate
Shine soft, and clear:
Thou mayest wait.

No longer shall we see
Thee walking in the crowded streets,
But where the ocean of the Future beats
Against the floodgates of the Present, swirling to this earth.
Another birth
Thou mayest have;
Another Arcady
May thee receive.

Not here thou dost remain,
Thou art gone far away,
Where, at the portals of the day,
The hours ever dance in ring, a silvern-footed throng,
While Time looks on,
And seraphs stand
Choiring an endless strain
On either hand.

Thou canst return no more;
Not as the happy time of spring
Comes after winter burgeoning
On wood and wold in folds of living green, for thou art
    dead.
Our tears we shed
In vain, for thou
Dost pace another shore,
Untroubled now.

FOUNDER'S ODE.

O SCHOLAR SAINT, who wore fair England's crown,
   And found it wrought of thorn,
O royal founder, come from Heaven down
   On this thy natal morn
To tread these cloister courts, where thou shalt find
   Thou didst not live in vain.
Not to no purpose did thy pious mind
   Design this fair domain.
Not to no purpose was thy sinless life
   Liv'd amid clash of arms.
A man of peace wast thou, for all thy strife
   And all dread war's alarms.
Thy life to all a failure seemed, no ray
   From fickle fortune shone—
Gone was thy Kingdom, vanish'd in a day,
   Thy royal power, gone.
So in the gloomy Tower wert thou cast,
   And darksome was the night,
And long and sad and weary to be passed
   Until the morning light.
The longest nights must have a dawn, and so
   At dawn thy spirit fled,
And up beyond this weary world of woe,
   O happy to be dead!

For thou behind thee here didst leave on earth
  A monument sublime,
A home of learning, happiness and mirth
  Untouched by hand of Time.
This thy memorial better far than those
  Which other Kings did raise;
This thy memorial, England's reddest Rose,
  Thy glory and our praise.
Thou hadst the treasure which by moth and rust
  Cannot corrupted be;
While others' tombstones crumble into dust
  We will remember thee.

TWO SONNETS.

I.

TO A. G. L.

BRIGHT flowers of a thousand hues I twin'd,
Watered by tears, yest're'en above thy door.
Tears are the fruit that Love in travail bore,
Sighs in the heart and anguish in the mind.
And as I twined I said, "The twilight nears;
Lose not your blossom, till the evening dies,
And when She passes forth, fall in suchwise
To damp her head with my fast-dropping tears."
Tomorrow I return; but if, at night
I should behold thee with faint footstep light
Mocking me with thy shadowiness in a dream,
Drunk with false pleasure, I shall not return.
No longer for the living shall I yearn;
My comfort be delights that only seem!

II.

TO A NIGHTINGALE.

THOU drink'st the fairy dew within the glade,
Thou singest within the wood by night and day,
With fluttering wings thou sing'st a roundelay,
A woodland carol for thy pleasure made.
For me, my songs are other songs than thine,
Though I sing here, I sing in different wise;
My song I veil about with plaintive sighs,
My soul with dropping tears I intertwine.
Thou sing'st for a short space: I sing for long:
The changing year re-echoes to my song.
My lady holds me in harsh servitude,
So, Philomel, or with my melody
(If Passion move thee) sing in harmony,
Or leave me lonely, weeping in the wood.

A PICTURE.

She sat within the dappling shade
That flickered o'er the forest glade,
The listening birches shadows made.

In that still place there was no stir,
About her fell the hair of her
Heavy with aloes and with myrrh.

A golden chain her waist confined,
Closed were her eyes, as she were blind.
Her robe was all with crimson lined,

With twisted cords about the hem,
Her wrists were twined with many a gem,
Her neck was like a lily stem.

About her feet a dragon slept,
His head upon her lap she kept
And while she guarded it, she wept.

Blind, anguished tears went dropping down
Upon the dragon's glassy crown,
Upon the margent of her gown.

Tall columbines grew 'mid the grass,
Between them shadow-mice did pass,
With soundless feet, pass and repass.

And, over all, the silence lay :
It seemed the evening of the day ;
It seemed the hour when all men pray.

So sate she still, this prison'd maid,
Within the lonely forest glade
Sate tending well the dragon's head.

Was she alive, and is she dead ?

TO CECILIA.

THY converse seems to me a garden close
    Where thick together spring
The pallent lily and the wine-dark rose,
And everything of fragrancy that grows,
    While argent voiced singers sing
    From every leaf-hung tree
Carols of faint and perfum'd loveliness,
Intwin'd with everliving mournfulness,
    In dappling greenery.

And so whene'er I speak with thee I seem
    So to be walking in some garden close,
A happy, faint and fragrant waking dream
Mix'd with the purling of a hidden stream
    Flowing along where purple iris grows.

AFTER THE FRENCH OF ESTIENNE DE LA BOETIE.

THE parching heat of the resplendent sun,
   Warming the whole earth with its golden ray,
Has touched with gold the ripening ear of corn.
   But we have waited all to-day
For the still freshness of the evening time,
     Margaret and I.

The sun has set, and now we wend our way
   At random through the rustling of the trees;
Before us Cupid strings his bow in play,
   And we two follow at our ease
Through the great silence of the starlit night,
     Margaret and I.

We are at peace with all. We do not care
   For King or royal court or rushing town;
But if we tire of the fresh forest air,
   We seek the meadows low adown
In the quiet valleys where the cowslips grow,
     Margaret and I.

O Médoc solitary, wild and free,
   Thou seemest ever perfect in my eyes;
Thou knowest all our present ills; in thee
   We'll live under thy clear blue skies
In peace, far distant from the world's wild waves,
     Margaret and I.

FANCY.

I WALKED in the wood at evening
   When the dew was on every tree,
And I saw in the darkness a lady
   Who looked from her casement on me.

And up to her tower of jacinth
   She drew me with eyes of flame:
And I was as one who slumbers,
   And knew not the way I came.

But down through a rift in the tree-tops
   A splinter of moonlight shone,
And I saw the eyes of that lady—
   I saw that her soul was gone.

IN MEMORIAM.

A DULL grey sky that hangs above,
A dull grey earth that sleeps beneath,
A vast grey wall around, the clouds of death,
Numbing my senses all. I cannot move:
My eyes are dim: and every sound
Seems as the murmur of a far-off waterfall,
That plunges down amid the sighing trees
Unseen, unknown: and all around
The deathly stillness of that gloomy pall,
That every joyous thought doth grimly seize
And crush within the grip of cold Despair,
Which lowering broods upon the stagnant air.

Nought there to see, and nought to feel
Save how the sword of misery
Doth stab and stab again unceasingly:
Nor aught the gaping wound can ever heal
For he is gone, for he is dead.
He died for home and freedom, but he died, he died
And we shall see his well-belovèd face
No more: no more the well-known tread
Shall hear; no more shall haply sit beside
The crackling fire and listen for a space
To that dear voice; nor through the woods at eve
Shall roam and every thought of sadness leave.

Shall we not mourn for one so dear?
　　O God of battles, God of love,
　Why dost Thou snatch to Thy bright realms above
　So swiftly those whose love we treasure here?
　　For all our love doth seem in vain,
When it at last a dwelling place secure doth find,
　If straightway by the hand of cruel Death
　　'Tis rudely crushed, and thrust away again.
　For though our strength doth fade, our eyes grow blind,
　The ghost of murdered love will ever breathe
　His whispered words of sorrow in the heart,
　Nor suffer sad sweet memory to part.

THOUGHTS.

O THOUGHTS, vain thoughts that ever wayward fly,
  Nor pause before the hallowed ground ye tread,
  But enter in to chase some vision dread
  Of wondrous loveliness : yet bye and bye
Ye must return to this poor world, and fall, and die.
  Then only for a space : ye flee
  Once more, when sweetest harmony
Floats on the air : once more your course is sped :
  Or when the scent of summer flowers
  With fragrance fills the sunlit bowers
  With roses decked, and marigold,
That nestle 'neath the spreading beeches old.

LINES ON HEARING BEETHOVEN'S "MOONLIGHT" SONATA.

I STOOD upon the heaven-aspiring height
   Of an aerial mountain, that had piled
   Its massive bluffs and precipices wild
Into one towering peak: the waning light
Dimly revealed in deathlike sleep,
The rolling spurs below enrapt, and valleys deep.

Above me the vast clouds did slowly float
   In still array majestically gliding,
     Through which the radiant moon her course was guiding
Onward from rift to rift, as one lone boat
The long, long ocean swell doth breast,
While the red sun sinks slow adown the fiery West.

And as I gazed upon that awful scene,
   Deep wondrous thoughts within my heart grew fast,
   As if the mighty clouds therein had cast
Their shadows dim: so heaven and earth between
My spirit fluttered, and was filled
With strange and lovely joy, that all my being thrilled.

Yet soon my thoughts came back to me once more;
    And with a sigh I rose, and turned away
    Down to the wooded slopes, that seemed to say,
" Return, return; thy heavenly dream is o'er."
And so with light steps I descended,
Happy, yet sad for that the glorious hour was ended.

And now the stars shone brighter: from the woods
    Astir with all their nightly revelry
    A myriad murmurs rose enchantingly:
The last sweet fragrance stole from closing buds;
And all who through the drowsy day
Had slept, came out beneath the cold bright moon to play.

So wonderingly I passed adown the hill,
    When suddenly reechoed through the night
    A peal of thunder, and the craggy height,
Which late had been so calm, and clear, and still,
Turning I saw all darkly clouded
And in a curtain black of grey whirling mists enshrouded.

And here and there amid the gathering storm
    The black and frowning crags stood grimly forth;
    And the wind shrieked in fierce and furious wrath,
While lightnings dazzling paths of fire did form.
    So the great tempest raged, and passed:
And through the thundering chasms at the last
Rolled muttering o'er the hills one long, low dying blast.

TO R. W., 1915.

HIGH over a wooded valley,
   And over a river fair,
Where childhood reigned unquestioned,
   God's peace lay there.

In his soul in early manhood,
   Before he received his share
Of his dear country's burden,
   God's peace lay there.

In the land wherein he lieth,
   Free from sorrow and from care,
'Neath Nature's verdant mantle:
   God's peace lies there!

DEATH.

O Death, thou uninvited guest,
Yet best belov'd of those whose quest
Is God's own peace and perfect rest—
　Why fear thee?

ON AN EARLY MORNING FUNERAL IN AMIENS CATHEDRAL.

In the morning white they paced,
  Bearing forth that holy thing,
'Neath the columns interlaced
  Of the high Cathedral nave:
While the solemn priests did sing,
  And their music, wave on wave,
Beat against the emblazoning
  Of the vast concave.

Forth into the snowy way
  Fragrant with the mist of night,
By the timid primal ray
  That sad burthen they have borne:
And the glimmering tapers' light
  Battles with the infant morn,
But the burthen seems more white
  Than the white of dawn.

BEGGARS IN LYONESSE.
I.

The beauty of spring lilies
  Is fine and white and gold;
Waving daffodilies
  Have been sung of old;
Blood and snow of roses
  Anyone can praise,
Or poppy that uncloses
  In the sun's hot rays.

Be the waving glory
  Of thy tresses bright
This poor singer's story,
  And the virgin white
Of thy bosom's heaving:
  But thy lips and eyes
They are past believing—
  They are God's first lies.

II.

GOD has not given me
   Music to charm men's ears,
I cannot offer thee
   Ten thousand deathless years.
Not on my wings of song
   Down the great Future stream
Shalt thou be borne along,
   Idle is all my dream.

Thou on great eagle's wing
   Wingest thy way through time;
All that all poets sing
   Is thine uplifting rhyme.
Poor thief, from their bright gold
   I steal to crown thy head:
Oh, rapture all untold
   So to be garlanded.

God upon thee did shower
   Bounteous, so rare a prize
That it were in thy power
   Me to immortalize.
Thou hast no need of more:
   Would he had given me
Out of his golden store
   Something to offer thee.

LE SUICIDE.

O FOREST-BROWNED, blue water-pool
   And glade scarce lit by sun :
Ye have bewitched a wandering fool,
   Sore evil have ye done.

Distraught he wandered seeking grace
   From God in Heaven : but ye
Did snatch him to your hiding-place
   And stole his soul from me.

Ye sent him forth at eventide
   Nor man nor half a man,
Save in the fleshly form outside
   His soul was 'neath God's ban.

Ye thrust him forth, ye bade him, " Walk
   In freedom through the earth."
And lo ! a living grave I stalk,
   Awaiting my new birth.

For death alone my cruel pangs
   (Death is new birth) can heal.
In life is godless weariness,
   In death is god-sent weal.

O forest-browned, blue water-pool,
   O glade that 'scap'st the sun,
Ye have betrayed a wandering fool,
   Foul murder have ye done.

LINES.

Within my narrow bed I lie,
And watch the hours go swiftly by
Reflected in a patch of sky.

At early morn it is a chink
Of softest delicatest pink,
Wherein cloud wavelets heave and sink.

At the third hour a gentle blue
Delicious, moist with morning dew
Tells me the world's awake anew.

But cruel noon with heartless glare
Kills all the freshness in the air
And cowes my gaze with angry stare.

Then as the hours press on, it seems
The wind is fraught with wistful dreams;
Flow through the air voluptuous streams,

Scenting the earth, then pomped West
Marshals her royal lord to rest,
And lays his head in her soft breast.

Warmth dies. The sanctuary light
Flickers and fades before the night.
The world is curtained from my sight.

THE HOMECOMING.

From the depth of the dreamy vale, from the height of the topmost mount,
Swift as leaves in the gale, numberless (who could count?)
A thousand thousand shades o'er the starlight country glide,
As the lampèd evening fades, and day is stripped of his pride.

Ask of them whither they go, ask of them whence are they bound,
Never a glance will show, never an answering sound;
Only a passing breeze will echo a voice full low
In and among the trees, " Homewards ever we go."

THE HOMECOMING:
A Second interpretation.

SEE! across the angry sky
How God's messenger doth fly,
Michael with the sword of flame;
(Christ preserve our souls from shame!)

How the firmament is red:
Restless seas give up their dead:
Corse uplifts his withered frame:
(Christ preserve our souls from shame!)

This the day of awful fame:
(Christ preserve our souls from shame!)
Speak, O dweller on the Throne,
Is our home Thine own, Thine own?

IN MEMORIAM.

When Christ took flesh and blood, and in them wrapped
   The glory of His high Divinity,
   And, from His place within the Trinity,
Came to a world in sinful meshes trapped

And cut them loose, men gave Him then a crown
   Wrought of rich thorns, yet so He loved it well,
   Dear symbol of His victory over Hell
For which alone to earth He was come down.

And later He ascended; still mankind
   Thought it was right that they should wreathe His brow
   With a bright circlet: yet not thorny now
They wrought it, but from out its gold-work shined

Diamond and pearl, sapphire and sardonyx,
   Jacinth and opal, glimmering emerault
   Set in massed gold, gems without taint or fault.
" What circlet this or who therein did fix

So wondrous gems, such wealth of yellow gold?"
　The Spirit saith: " O loved of Christ, this crown
　Is His dear Church; these gems of high renown,
Which thy dull eyes of earth can scarce behold,

His saints in glory: She whom thou dost seek,
　Though new her place, yet brightly here doth gleam.
　Bend low thy knees in worship: else the theme
Too high shall be: Worship or dare not speak."

LITERARY FANCIES.

ONE.

O, I would have a ballad old,
With my love mured up in a baron's hold,
  And I so gay to steal her away,
And crown her my queen with a crown of gold,
  And merrymen singing a roundelay.

TWO.

O, I would have some rhymster's feat
With many a play and a quaint conceit,
  And I so fine to pass round the wine
With a jest so pat and a quip so neat,
  Till all should swear there be none like mine.

THREE.

O, I would have a playbook rare
And none of your rhymes and your coarser fare,
  But sitting alone in state on my throne,
To hold my court, and rule with care,
  And have all Christendom for my own.

FOUR.

O, I would have a fairy tale
And queen it all in a shady vale.
  And I myself, with a page-boy elf,
To witch the wicked and turn them pale
  And richen the poor with their ill-gained pelf.

SUMMER.

I saw Summer dancing in the sunlight,
   And the little breezes laughing in her hair;
Tall as a goddess with the scent of flowers
   Straying all around her—O, but she was fair !

Slender her neck was, and white as any lily,
   Ruddy her lips were, and fit to shame a rose;
And all the glory, and the joy of living,
   Laughed in the grace that only summer knows.

Then there came Autumn sombrely apparelled,
   Chasing the golden Summer from her play;
Now all is dreary, and my world is darkened,
   Summer, Summer dearest, since thou'rt fled away.

MY HOME.

The house that I'd have would be in the hollow
   That made a dimple on some mountain's cheek,
Where, up above me, racing winds would follow
   Winds, in a boist'rous game of hide-and-seek.

There'd be my home, and fir trees would surround it,
   Standing on guard there, black, and bleak, and bare;
There'd be a garden, and a wall around it,
   And all my favourite flowers would be there.

There would I live, as far from the commotion
   Of city life, and of the crowded street,
As I should be in desert or mid-ocean,
   Nor heed the noise of ever-hurrying feet.

REQUIESCAM.

Let me lie in peace at last,
When the whirl of life is past,
On Thy mercy, Lord, be cast:
    For this I pray.

More than this I do not crave,
Nor a place among the brave,
But at night to find my grave
    Until the Day.

NEC QUAE PRAETERIT, HORA REDIRE POTEST.

YET another day is past,
　Darkness comes again;
Grant it may not be my last:
　It was spent in vain.

BEATUS ILLE.

A LITTLE garden in a town :
   A pergola which shivers
      When the trains go by :
A spacious park whose lawns slope down
   To views of silent rivers
      Or of hillsides high.

Happy may be the lord
   Who on his terrace seat reposes :
      But blind and wretched if he mocks,
As he gazes on his lands so broad,
   At a quarter-acre full of roses
      And August holly-hocks.

THE PRISONER.

BLIND are my eyes that darkness grope,
  And deaf the ears I strain to hear,
And every step without, a hope,
  And every little noise a fear,
  And yet she cannot but be near.

Light will she come, who nothing fears,
  But they with heavy tread, and slow,
And every voice without is hers,
  And every step, the step I know,
  Ah God! if it should not be so!

I feel the clammy wall, and dank,
  I feel the chains; my wrists are bound;
I dare not move me lest they clank,
  And senseless terror clings me round,
  I clutch my senses lest thy swound.

I feel the sun is sinking low:
  O day, that I have never seen,
You fade without. She cannot know,
  'Tis best that she live on, a queen,
  Careless as I had never been.

LIFE.

LIFE is a picture-book of many pages,
   And on each page there is a picture set
By different actors played on different stages
   Scenes worthy to remember or forget.

There is a single figure running through it,
   With just your face, the servant of your brain:
'Tis yours to guide; be careful how you do it:
   You cannot read the book of life again.

VALE.

O MOTHER, I go forth to see
   The old things of the world, and new,
And all that you have made of me,
   And all that I have made of you
I take to prove my fealty,
   And pay you honour due.

You are immortal as your sons
   Immortal are; they owed to you
The seed of higher things that once
   You sowed in soil so new,
A tale that he may read, who runs,
   Of all they found to do.

What though my labour feeble seems
   In thee: forth go I, to make known,
If falsely fair my future gleams.
   And all those hopes were hopes alone,
And all those dreams were only dreams,
   Which first you gave me for my own.

You, that have cast your lot in me,
   And me upon the waters face,
If aught I own of loyalty,
   Shall find me after many days,
Striving with all my best to be
   Worthy of all your love and grace.